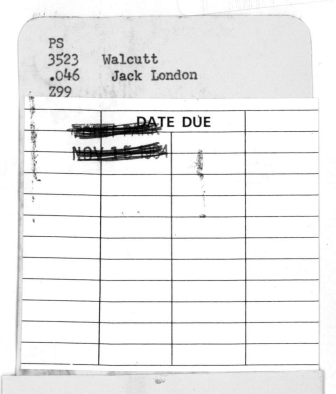

POINT PARK COLLEGE
Wood St. and Blvd. of Allies
Pittsburgh 22, Pa.

PRINTED IN U.S.A.

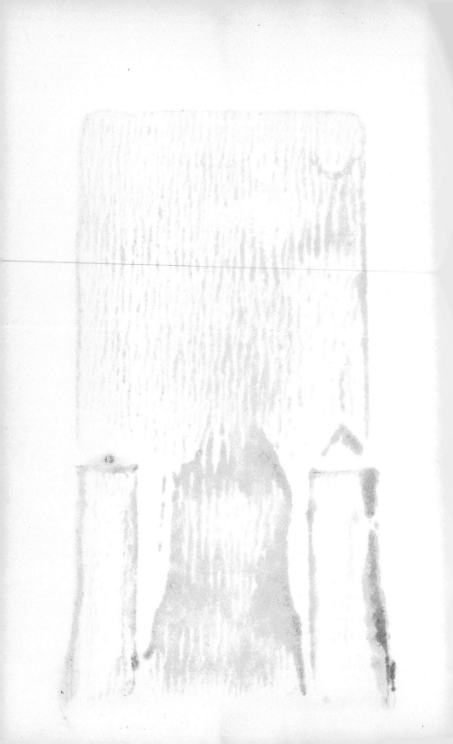

UNIVERSITY OF MINNESOTA

.65

Jack London

BY CHARLES CHILD WALCUTT

PS
3523
.O46
Z 99

8118/67

Aloner

UNIVERSITY OF MINNESOTA PRESS · MINNEAPOLIS

JACK LONDON

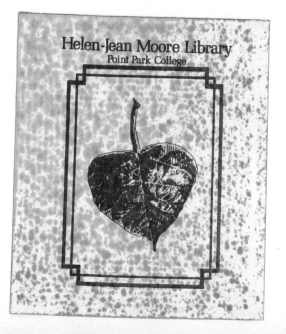

CHARLES CHILD WALCUTT is the author of numerous books, among them *Man's Changing Mask: Modes and Methods of Characterization in Fiction* and *American Literary Naturalism, a Divided Stream*. He teaches at Queens College and the City University of New York.

↲ *Jack London*

J ACK LONDON lived (1876–1916) at a time when a dramatically new set of ideas, growing out of the theory of evolution, was changing the course of men's thinking. These ideas stimulated, frustrated, and tantalized London all his adult years. Charles Darwin and Herbert Spencer, messiahs of the new creed, became his intellectual mentors, along with Friedrich Nietzsche and Karl Marx. It might be said that London's very real private struggle with life — which he dramatized in stories so arresting and exciting that they are still read over the world — became for him an epitome of the Darwinian Struggle for Existence, his success an example of the Spencerian Survival of the Fittest.

It is not easy for people today, who have lived with accelerating change through two-thirds of the twentieth century, to grasp how revolutionary and shattering were Darwin's and Spencer's ideas. Before they burst upon the intellectual horizon it was, for example, generally held that the world had been created in precisely the year 4004 B.C. and that the various species of flora and fauna were immutable: a rose, or a horse, or a man had always been the same creature, although variations or developments *within* each kind were possible. Then came Darwin in 1859 to propose that the earth was many millions of years old and that all extant species had evolved from a common beginning in the sea at some remote moment of time. Design and order had not presided over this evolution, either; it took place through the accumulation of infinitesimal and accidental variations. Millions upon millions of individuals (in whatever species) were wasted in the struggle for existence in which the slightly superior variation managed to survive and reproduce itself. The first reaction to this great theory was outrage. Darwin was denounced from countless Christian pulpits by ministers who accused him of maintaining that man descended from monkeys — although this was one point that he did not urge in his *Origin of Species*. Even so, the implication was unmistakable, and the very foundations of religion seemed to be threatened.

If Darwin was the scientist of evolution, Herbert Spencer was its philosopher. He worked from 1860 to 1903 on the many volumes of his great *Synthetic Philosophy*, a work that undertook a new synthesis of knowledge based on a new guiding idea, which was, of course, evolution. Spencer asserted that evolution is the fundamental law of social as well as physical process: from simple and relatively uniform materials evolve increasingly complex and specialized structures. He contended that the more complex forms, whether individual creatures or social organizations, are the more stable — and thus he saw the social struggle for existence as leading up to the ultimately perfect and stable society. The evils of child labor, poverty, unemployment, and industrial warfare which were rampant in Western Europe and America were justified because they were the means to that perfect society. The fit would survive. Every social and industrial violence, every outrage caused by competition, was beatified with an aura of destined good in the philosophy of Social Darwinism. This put the humanitarianism and idealism of the nineteenth century under a frightful strain. The blessed prospect of the perfect society springing from child labor called for specially tinted lenses.

For many, a central figure in the social struggle came to be the "superman." In his ruthless quest for power this giant among men would help along the selection of the fittest by crushing the weak and helpless. The superman so appealed to Spencerian thinking that surely he would have been invented by someone else if the

6

German philosopher Nietzsche had not done so. In fact the term "superman" by itself had the power to inflame the imaginations of many who had never read *Thus Spake Zarathustra*, and the rugged individualist supermen that emerged in popular literature — often ferocious blond Vikings — bore small resemblance to the type of genius Nietzsche described.

At the same time the role of unbridled individualism in the evolution of society was being challenged by the philosophy of socialism. In *The Communist Manifesto* Karl Marx had called upon the workingmen of the world — the supposedly weak and helpless victims of natural selection — to unite and overthrow their exploiters and oppressors, the industrialist ruling classes. According to the followers of Marx, not the superman individualist but the socialist community of workers must be the instrument of evolutionary progress.

It was this complex of ideas, contradictions and all, that captured the strong but untutored mind of young Jack London and permeated his writing. If we look briefly at his early trials in a world of extremes in wealth and poverty, in opportunity and helplessness, we may be led to understand how he came to fight — in his private life and in his work — up and down the line between Social Darwinism and social justice, between individualism and socialism. He had the physical and intellectual powers to make him identify with the superman sweeping lesser beings out of his way in the upward climb to the perfect society; at the same time he had both the experience of privation and the capacity for sympathy to make him take up the cause of all the hapless waifs crushed under a ruthless industrial juggernaut. He was inspired by the American dream of success even while he was living among the most oppressed of outcasts.

London was the offspring of a strange union between Flora Wellman and "Professor" W. H. Chaney. Flora came of sturdy

Welsh stock, but she had been stricken by typhus in her girlhood and afterwards she was unstable if not unbalanced. Chaney was an itinerant intellectual who made all knowledge his province and apparently remembered everything he had ever read. He always denied the paternity of Jack London, but the evidence of physical appearance and intellectual quality seems to be undeniable. Irving Stone, biographer of London who made considerable study of Chaney's writings, reports that they reveal "a clear, forceful, and pleasing literary style, an authentic erudition, courage to speak his mind, a sympathy for the mass of humanity, and a desire to teach them to better themselves. His point of view is modern and progressive." Chaney believed that a proper use of astrology would enable mankind finally to improve the human condition.

Flora was an ardent spiritualist, and séances were offered along with lectures on astrology and spiritualism while she and Chaney were living together, from June 1874 to June 1875. Flora wanted marriage and a child, but Chaney was too distressed by her violent temper to consider a permanent union; when she declared that she was pregnant by him and he denied responsibility, she either genuinely attempted to commit suicide or pretended to do so. In any event, Chaney was denounced and ostracized, even by his own family. Flora gave birth to a son on January 12, 1876, in San Francisco. Eight months later she married John London and named her child for him, John Griffith London.

John London went into one business after another in California. Although he was a man of character and determination, he was repeatedly ruined, sometimes by the scoundrelism of a partner or, more typically, by the irresponsible plans of Flora. Young Jack lived from hand to mouth, getting a spotty primary education and working at one job after another to help his indigent family, which finally settled in Oakland. When he was thirteen he bought a small boat and learned to sail on San Francisco Bay. A year or so later, out of school, he got a larger boat and became an expert sailor. But just when freedom seemed within his grasp, John London was injured and Jack became the mainstay of the family. He supported this crushing load by becoming an oyster pirate — one of a gang of small boat owners who raided the oyster beds in the dark of night and sold what they stole to markets and saloons in San Francisco. On his first raid he made as much money as he had been earning in three months of "legitimate" toil.

Jack had a young mistress on his oyster boat, the *Razzle Dazzle*. He also began at the age of fifteen to drink very heavily and nearly killed himself in the process. At the same time he was devouring books taken from the Oakland library. From oyster pirate he became a member of the State Fish Patrol, whose duty it was to arrest illegal fishermen. At seventeen he shipped on a sealing vessel, the *Sophie Sutherland*. After seven months on the Pacific he returned to California and worked about a year at common labor for miserable wages (the Panic of 1893 had caused widespread unemployment, depressing wages). London then joined the march on Washington of Kelly's Industrial Army, which planned to join forces with Coxey's Army in the East to demand government aid for the jobless. His affiliation with the Army was rather loose, for he acted as a self-appointed advance guard, arriving in town ahead of the Army and living in solid comfort for a day or so while the residents debated how to welcome (or rebuff) the main force when it appeared. The march on Washington failed, and London became a hobo. He served time in prison for vagrancy and saw the seamiest side of American life before making his way back to California.

Determined to prepare himself for better than common labor, he entered Oakland High School when he was nineteen. He published in the school magazine, made interesting friends, and through the Henry Clay Debating Society was put in touch with a widening circle of stimulating people. He had become an avowed socialist, however, and when he was thrown in jail for speaking in a park without a license he found that many of his more prosperous new acquaintances drew back. The newspapers reported on him as if he were a combination of devil and maniac. In 1896, after a summer of merciless cramming (nineteen hours a day, according to him), he passed the entrance examinations and entered the University of California. There he was popular in a small circle of students and seemed happy, but life never left London in peace. After a single semester he had to leave and go back to work to support his parents, John London's health having failed. But first he had a heroic go (fifteen hours a day) at writing, turning out stories, poetry, essays, and tracts and sending them east with his last pennies. The manuscripts all came back. Jack went to work. After some months of exhausting physical labor he borrowed a considerable sum of money from his stepsister Eliza and embarked for the Klondike in March 1897.

London came home a year later without an ounce of gold but with head and notebook full of plans for stories. It turned out to be the most valuable period of his life. He wrote like a man possessed, gaunt, hungry, twitching. This time he found success. In May, June, and July 1899 his stories and articles appeared in the *Overland Monthly, Orange Judd Farmer, Black Cat, Buffalo Express, Home Magazine, American Journal of Education,* and *The Owl.* In December the *Atlantic Monthly* accepted a long story for the princely sum of $120, and Houghton, Mifflin shortly afterwards contracted to publish a volume of short stories. At the same time London was avidly reading and taking notes on the best writers in the new sciences of nature, man, and society. His dedication to the enlightenment of man and the cause of socialism was terribly earnest and people felt his strength and his sincerity; he made many friends and impressed whomever he met. He and his mother (John London had died) moved into a large house in Oakland that became a center of social, intellectual, and roistering activities; old friends from the sea and the road rubbed elbows with writers, philosophers, anarchists, and literary highbrows.

Three critical events took place in the spring and the summer of 1900. His stories appeared in book form as *The Son of the Wolf* and won extraordinary acclaim. Editor-publisher S. S. McClure asked to become his literary sponsor and took a steady flow of his stories for good prices; McClure also agreed to advance the young author $125 a month while he wrote his first novel. And London gave up the girl he had been courting, Mabel Applegarth, whose mother dominated her and promised to dominate the marriage, and married instead Bessie Maddern. This turned out to be a leap from the frying pan into the fire, for London's mother, the neurotic Flora, now proceeded to make home a hell as she battled with Bess for control of the premises. Moving Flora into a separate house added to London's expenses without solving the problem, for she promptly laid siege to the main house, carried the campaign to the neighbors, and went back to her old business schemes — making new debts for her son.

McClure's "salary" was stopped after October 1901 because the editor did not find London's output holding up to the quality he had expected. But still London's reputation was growing. Macmillan accepted a volume of stories about the Indians of Alaska, *Children of the Frost* (1902). He turned out two juveniles, *The Cruise of the Dazzler* (1902) and *Tales of the Fish Patrol* (1905). Lippincott published his first novel, *A Daughter of the Snows* (1902). He worked with one of his few platonic women friends, Anna Strunsky, on a volume called *The Kempton-Wace Letters* (1903) in which he took the scientific-intellectual point of view on various topics and she the romantic-aesthetic position. He set out for South Africa in 1902 to report the Boer War for the

American Press Association. When he arrived in London en route to find a cable canceling the assignment, he bought himself shabby old clothes and plunged into London's East End where humanity languished in one of its lowest depths. From his observations he wrote in the three months he was there *The People of the Abyss*, a powerful image of misery. "Year by year rural England pours in a flood of vigorous young life that perishes by the third generation. At all times four hundred and fifty thousand human creatures are dying miserably at the bottom of the social pit called London." When he landed in New York, George Brett, head of the Macmillan Company, promptly accepted the manuscript and agreed to pay London $150 a month for two years while he wrote the novels that he was now confident about.

This was only the beginning. Home in California, he was inspired to write a dog story. What he began as a short story grew and grew until it became *The Call of the Wild*. Macmillan gave him $2000 for all rights to the book in lieu of royalties — much more than London had ever made from a book or expected to make in the near future. By 1900 standards it was more than a generous income for a year. To London, who scarcely three years before had been pleading in vain for five dollars which the *Overland Monthly* had promised him for "To the Man on Trail," it was a fortune. He was happy to accept the offer. Macmillan made a fantastic profit on the arrangement: well over two million copies of the English edition alone have been sold. Even so, it was for the best. According to Irving Stone, "No less than a hundred people a week walked through his front door, enjoyed his hospitality," and occupied his time. It was his salvation to have cash to buy a good sloop on which he could disappear for weeks at a time to write in peace. London also received a substantial sum for *The Call of the Wild* from the *Saturday Evening Post*, which serialized it.

The pattern of prodigious success and prodigious spending was now set. *The Call of the Wild* (1903) was immediately declared a classic. Serialization of *The Sea-Wolf* (1904) brought $4000 from *Century* magazine, and the book sold forty thousand copies in advance of publication. Three weeks after publication it topped the best-seller list. These books plus *The People of the Abyss* (1903) and *The War of the Classes* (1905) were on everybody's lips. Also topics of widespread interest were London's ardent preaching of socialism, his divorce from Bessie in 1905, and his marriage to Charmian Kittredge two days later. He bought a large ranch in California and planned to cruise around the world for seven years, on a ketch to be called the *Snark*, while the ranch's crops were developing. He burned his way through *Before Adam* (1907), going back to the dawn of humanity, and *The Iron Heel* (1907), jumping prophetically forward seven hundred years to a Marxist analysis of the triumph of fascism. Meanwhile he had decided to build the forty-five-foot *Snark* himself, a decision that proved the costliest of his life up to this point. He poured between $30,000 and $50,000 into a boat that was not as good as one he could have bought for $5000. He was cheated and victimized; and yet one cannot escape the impression that he created many of his own troubles. Sailing time was repeatedly put off but finally he limped out of San Francisco Bay in a boat that had been crushed, foundered in mud, almost sunk — and was still far from finished — limped off in worse debt than ever before. The chaotic voyage lasted over two years, taking London to Hawaii, the Marquesas, Tahiti, and Australia, and among other troubles it came very close to ruining his health. Yet during the course of it he wrote a long novel, *Martin Eden* (1909), also *Adventure* (1911), and many stories. Returning to San Francisco in July 1909, his business affairs in a desperate state and his literary reputation at low ebb, he plunged into another nineteen-hour-a-day orgy of

13

work to rehabilitate himself. He came back so strongly that by 1911 he was again earning hugely and enjoying renewed critical acclaim. And again he plunged into new buying and building.

London's land holdings increased in a few years to fifteen hundred acres; he employed more than a hundred people, with a payroll of $3000 a month. While a stone dream palace was a-building, he had a great house called Beauty Ranch reconditioned and set up as a mecca for the guests from all over the world who daily poured into the Glen Ellen station, took the wagon that met every train, and enjoyed the Master's hospitality while they contributed to his knowledge of human nature. He impressed visitors of every level as one of the most brilliant minds they had ever encountered. At the same time he was steadily writing a thousand words a day, with contracts for everything he could turn out. Earning $75,000 a year, he was never less than $25,000 in debt and often $50,000: he was panhandled by acquaintances, milked by people he had never met, cheated by friends who were handling his affairs or his money, and robbed by his employees.

A climax came in 1913 when his magnificent dream castle, called Wolf House, built over four years at a cost of perhaps $100,000, was destroyed by fire shortly before the Londons were to move into it. Someone had apparently done it deliberately — and it was uninsured. During the same year London published *The Night-Born*, *The Abysmal Brute*, *John Barleycorn*, *The Valley of the Moon*, and *The Scarlet Plague* (in serial form), completed *The Mutiny of the Elsinore* (1914), and began *The Star Rover* (1915). But his faith in man was shaken, his drinking increased with his debts, drought ruined his crops, disease plagued his stock, and his own health was failing.

During his last three years he became more businessman and less artist. He said to a young interviewer, "I dream of beautiful horses and fine soil. I dream of the beautiful things I own . . . And I

14

write for no other purpose than to add to the beauty that now belongs to me. I write a book for no other reason than to add three or four hundred acres to my magnificent estate." He was more renowned now for husbandry than for his writing; he laid plans to revitalize California stock breeding and agriculture by scientific methods. He did not care about his debts because he was sure that he was creating a self-sufficient empire at Glen Ellen where he could defy the world. Irving Stone says that he was "a modest megalomaniac, like most native Californians"! His latest biographer, Richard O'Connor, says, "He was gypped, hoodwinked, overcharged and outbargained wherever he went, but the illusion of fiscal capability would not die. Like Mark Twain, and along much the same lines, he was tempted to beat the businessmen at their own game and make himself independent of any income from writing."

But the writing still paid. In April 1914, when the United States was landing troops at Vera Cruz, he was offered $1100 a week by *Collier's* to report events in Mexico. There the pacifist-socialist revealed a changing face. He admired the American army and navy, affirmed that war was fundamental to the human condition, and took the side of American oil interests against the Mexican freedom fighters whom he saw as simply bandits and robbers. He was roused by World War I to declare that Germany was a mad nation that should be destroyed at any cost. Disillusioned with socialism, he now resigned from the party because it blamed the war on international capitalism rather than on Germany.

Increasingly London became a man yearning for the past. His greatest literary resource was, after all, the Klondike. As it receded from the public mind, London found himself falling behind Harold Bell Wright as an entertainer and Theodore Dreiser as avant-garde. He found Charmian increasingly possessive, jealous, childish. But worst of all he was very sick: constant headaches,

CHARLES CHILD WALCUTT

agonizing uremia and nephritis, rheumatism, dysentery, and
excess weight — all apparently due to his heavy drinking and vora
cious eating. He died from an overdose of narcotics. It was not a
premeditated suicide, for he had gone to bed after making plan
for the morrow, but apparently an attack of uremia brought more
pain than he could bear, and he took the fatal dose in order to
escape. At forty he had written fifty books and piled up a burden
of debt and illness that he could carry no further.

London's Klondike stories brought strong praise; he was called
the successor to Poe, the equal of Kipling, a new voice rising above
the prissy sentiment of the genteel tradition. The best of his storie
have extraordinary power, which is generated by bold ideas, vigor
and concreteness of language, and that combination of mystery
and suspense that is the mark of the born storyteller. London
jumps into the middle of his situation; he keeps the reader on
tenterhooks by withholding facts in a way that makes him par
ticipate in the action.

One of London's earliest stories, "The White Silence," written
in 1898, published in February 1899 in the *Overland Monthly*
is typical of the best. It introduces the Malemute Kid and his pal
Mason, caught two hundred miles from town in weather sixty-five
degrees below zero with starving dogs and inadequate food for
themselves. With them is Ruth, Mason's devoted Indian wife
carrying his child, sustained by the hope of seeing the white man's
great cities. They experience the White Silence: "All movement
ceases, the sky clears, the heavens are as brass; the slightest whisper
seems sacrilege, and man becomes timid, affrighted at the sound
of his own voice. Sole speck of life journeying across the ghostly
wastes of a dead world, he trembles at his audacity, realizes that
his is a maggot's life, nothing more." Mason is fatally injured by
a falling tree. If they wait for him to die, they will all die. He

insists that they go on. After a day of grim waiting, Malemute Kid sends the girl on ahead, shoots the dying man, and lashes the dogs into a wild gallop as he flees across the snow.

"To Build a Fire" (1908) describes in minutest detail a man in the same cold "The White Silence" describes, trying to build a fire to warm himself before he freezes to death. He does get a fire going, but underneath a spruce tree, and the snow falls off the tree and puts it out. Lighting it the second time is the ordeal; his toes are frozen, his fingers too numb to feel the match, and he does not quite make it. The cold rapidly closes in on him. Dreams and hallucinations flutter through his consciousness as the end comes near. The suspense builds to an intense pitch.

"Bâtard" (1902) is a rich concoction of raw elements. Bâtard is the son of a gray timber wolf and a "snarling, bickering, obscene, husky" bitch with "a genius for trickery and evil." Black Leclère buys this dog because he hates him and wants to torment him. But Bâtard had "his mother's tenacious grip on life. Nothing could kill him. He flourished under misfortune, grew fat with famine, and out of his terrible struggle for life developed a pre-ternatural intelligence. His were the stealth and cunning of the husky, his mother, and the fierceness and valor of the wolf, his father." Dog and master are bound by a savage hatred.

In their first major encounter, the dog leaps at Leclère's throat while he sleeps; the master disdains weapons, and in the ensuing fight they almost kill each other: "It was a primordial setting and a primordial scene, such as might have been in the savage youth of the world. An open space in a dark forest, a ring of grinning wolf-dogs, and in the centre two beasts, locked in combat, snapping and snarling, raging madly about, panting, sobbing, cursing, straining, wild with passion, in a fury of murder, ripping and tearing and clawing in elemental brutishness." Still the dog does not run away, and the master does not kill him, for they are

17

linked by their hatred. But the master torments him incredibly —
and with a reason: Bâtard invokes a subconscious death impulse
in Leclère: "Often the man felt that he had bucked against the
very essence of life — the unconquerable essence that swept the
hawk down out of the sky like a feathered thunderbolt, that drove
the great gray goose across the zones, that hurled the spawning
salmon through two thousand miles of boiling Yukon flood."

The climax is a masterpiece of fiendish savagery. And appalling
as it is, it is also convincing. The hate lives in London's intense
language; even if that language is somewhat extravagant — as it
certainly is — it convinces. It shows what it was that enthralled
his audience by outdoing readers' wildest dreams of adventure.
Perhaps the single word to describe it is energy: the writing renders
a fierce commitment to life. It was the quality that made London's
personal magnetism, and it vibrated in his prose.

The three volumes of his Yukon stories that appeared in 1900–
2 — *The Son of the Wolf, The God of His Fathers,* and *Children
of the Frost* — established his reputation. At the same time he was
turning to the novel form, in which his first try produced a tangle
of ideas that merits discussion. As he complained later, *A Daughter
of the Snows* (1902) contains enough material for several novels.
It has a lavish assortment of ideas. To begin with, London asserts
determinism: people's actions are the result of forces working
upon them. A man may run, "each new pressure prodding him as
he goes, until he dies, and his final form will be that predestined
of the many pressures." He celebrates primordialism, which is
another name for atavism; it is the notion that man's adaptability
depends upon his possession of primitive qualities that existed
before men became highly specialized and therefore incapable of
adapting to new challenges. There is also a subordination of
morals to survival. The superwoman heroine of the novel, Frona
Welse, glories in physical strength, obeys her own instincts, and

18

makes them the measure of what is good: "Why should she not love the body, and without shame?" Presently, however, these physical survival values are endowed with spiritual qualities: the choice of strength is a choice of good; weakness is evil; for it is the strong who will redeem mankind.

Now a set of ideas is one thing, but dramatizing them in a plotted action is quite another. The action here involves two suitors for the hand of Frona Welse. One is Gregory St. Vincent, who has already won her heart when Vance Corliss arrives in the frozen North, straight from the effeminacies of civilization, yet already responding atavistically to the challenge of the frontier. In order to create suspense, Frona must be blinded to the cowardice and treachery of St. Vincent, and Corliss must stand by heroically silent while she manifests her goodness by her loyalty (noble because misguided) to St. Vincent. Thus the action rests upon standard Victorian pieties. The moral order triumphs when St. Vincent is providentially exposed for the base creature he is, and Frona is free to pledge her heart and hand to Corliss. In the choices that, finally, determine characterization, Frona and Corliss are chaste, loyal, morally courageous, whereas St. Vincent is ruthless, selfish, and dominated by his impulses. These qualities should make him a perfect natural man, but in fact they make him the villain.

London was at the height of his powers in 1902 when he began writing the dog story which he thought of as balancing his account of the vicious husky given in "Bâtard." London finished *The Call of the Wild* in just over a month, his prose flowing pure and sharp with the story line, free from excessive expositions of intellectual theory.

Buck, a pleasant big dog, half Scotch shepherd, half St. Bernard, was stolen from his comfortable home in California and sold. Taken to the Yukon and put into brutal service in a dog team, he quickly learned the law of club and fang, learned that to survive in these arctic wilds he would have to be stronger and more cunning than other dogs on the team. His first big step was stealing a morsel of bacon from the other dogs. In this act his comfortable old morality was rejected as "a vain thing and a handicap in the ruthless struggle for existence," where respect for others might be suicidal. Soon he began to feel some savage atavism stirring his depths, and with the aurora borealis flaming overhead he joined in the old mournful song of the huskies, "old as the breed itself — one of the first songs of the younger world in a day when songs were sad." He fought with the leader of the team and took his place.

After several journeys, Buck was sold to another owner who was going to kill him when he was rescued and cared for by John Thornton. A great love grew between Buck and Thornton, and Buck more than once saved Thornton's life in camp and on the trail. Thornton almost brought Buck back to his old self, and perhaps he would have in time. But Thornton was murdered by Indians while Buck was chasing a moose. When Buck returned to find his dead master and the slayers, he raged through the camp like a thunderbolt, killing several Indians and wounding others. Then he fled into the wilderness, eventually becoming one of a wolf pack.

The story ends with a sentence that shows London at his best, a sentence that must have flowed in triumph from a writer who had come to the end of his purest book: "When the long winter nights come on and the wolves follow their meat into the lower valleys, he may be seen running at the head of the pack through the pale moonlight or glimmering borealis, leaping gigantic above his fellows, his great throat a-bellow as he sings a song of the younger world, which is the song of the pack."

At first glance *The Call of the Wild* seems to be entirely outside any traditional society and therefore free from its tensions, but in fact the narrative reveals various sorts of relations to the patterns of such a society. The values of love and fair play are central to the story; these are traditional and even heroic values. Buck begins happy and satisfied in a setting of comfort and love. Standard justice is betrayed when he is stolen and sold into bondage, but he rises to the challenge by drawing upon qualities of courage and hardihood. These are presented as atavistic, but they are also "moral" qualities that have always been respected in Western literature. And they are given new dignity when Buck responds to the love of John Thornton: the subordination of strength and courage to kindness and love is profoundly rooted in chivalry — which comes from the deep heart of Europe. Vengeance on the "inhuman" Indians who kill Thornton is chivalric too; it reaches back to the Crusades and beyond. So strong are these appeals, indeed, that one may feel a certain regret when Buck finally abandons human society.

Civilized man — especially American man — lives constantly with the call of the wild, but the call is quite different from the thing itself. The call represents the yearning toward freedom and purity that is an aspect of any human involvement; but one retreats in order to return with new strength. Robert Frost, climbing his birches to get away from it all, is very explicit:

> I'd like to get away from earth awhile
> And then come back to it and begin over.
> May no fate willfully misunderstand me
> And half grant what I wish and snatch me away
> Not to return. Earth's the right place for love . . .

If we substitute "society" for "earth" we have the same problem stated more literally. Buck represents the human qualities that are always somewhat sullied in the actual world; he represents revolt and escape; and he enacts his qualities in the story. Running at last, full-throated through the pale moonlight, exulting in his freedom and strength, he "sings a song of the younger world," which is the song of the American dream of innocence and Adamic purity, when man was fresh-minted and society had not bowed him down under its load of falsity. In this light, *The Call of the Wild* shines almost as a lyric rather than a novel. In any event, London here achieved an ideal fusion of form and subject. Since perfect escape is inhuman, it is not so extraordinary that his hero should be a dog.

Three years later London wrote *White Fang* (1906), a companion piece to *The Call of the Wild*. If in the first book he had shown a domestic dog reverting to wolf, the later one told how a wolf was domesticated. White Fang is three-fourths wolf and bred in the wild like a wolf. First he makes the "old covenant" between the wolf and man, which goes back to primitive times, by which the wolf adopts the man-god for protection and food while in turn he obeys and protects his master. White Fang's first covenant, with a harsh Indian, is based on instinct, fear, and respect but there is no love or affection. This covenant is broken during a great famine, restored when the wolf comes back, but broken forever when the master sells him for a bottle of liquor to a man who pits him against a bulldog, for money, and is willing to see him killed. In his second covenant, to his rescuer, White Fang gives himself wholly in love. He ends in just the sort of luxurious comfort that Buck enjoyed at the beginning of his story. *White Fang* is twice as long and perhaps not as bare, tense, and gripping as *The Call of the Wild*; but it is a powerful book.

In these two stories we can see the disguised and projected expression of London's contradictory theories of individualism and socialism. Buck is the individualist who defies society and finally rejects it completely. White Fang is tamed by love and turns from a savage wolf into a loving and home-keeping dog. This is the theory, but the impact of *White Fang* is still in violence, war, and survival by prowess. Most of the book concerns White Fang's struggles with savage nature, Indians, dogs, and white men, struggles that are as harsh as those of Buck in the first story. White Fang as clearly as Buck enacts London's own myth of a man unloved by his mother, unknown to his father, reared in poverty and deprivation, yet growing stronger and craftier because of innate powers that assert themselves and enable him to survive under extreme adversity.

The conclusion is prepared for by a vivid account of the experiences that molded White Fang's heredity while he was becoming fit to survive in the jungle of life: "Hated by his kind and by mankind, indomitable, perpetually warred upon and himself waging perpetual war, his development was rapid and one-sided. . . . The code he learned was to obey the strong and to oppress the weak. . . . He became quicker of movement than the other dogs, swifter of foot, craftier, deadlier, more lithe, more lean with iron-like muscle and sinew, more enduring, more cruel, more ferocious, and more intelligent. He had to become all these things, else he would not have held his own nor survived the hostile environment in which he found himself."

It is a wolf book, in short, and if at the end the wolf is tamed by love he is still a wolf. This merely reinforces one's conviction that London's heart was in individualism rather than socialism. His lip service to the latter is a protest against his early poverty; but he does not dwell on the presumed benefits of a socialist society. He writes instead of the evils of capitalism, the brutality of the industrial world, and the need for violent revolution to destroy them. The peace in his writing is the opulent peace of the great individualist who has beaten the system single-handed and can now afford to relax and live like a lord on his baronial domain. This is the peace of White Fang after he has conquered the world of club and fang by his prowess as a fighter. Near the end of the book White Fang kills a desperate murderer bent on destroying his master's father, thus showing the great power that is his, the power that he relaxes into love and ease but still keeps ready in case there is need for it in the treacherous world.

If White Fang ends where Buck was until he was stolen and sold into bondage, the lesson is that he must be stronger and smarter than Buck if he is to maintain his comfortable retirement in baronial splendor. This was London's dream of Wolf House — built of solid stone to outlast the ages while its master enjoyed the rewards of success. London loved to be called Wolf, signed his letters "Wolf," and had his bookmarks engraved with a picture of a wolf-dog's head. He wrote of animals as if they were people — and of people as if they were animals, recognizing no essential difference between human and animal societies.

White Fang begins with two men traveling through the arctic with dog team and sled, followed by a pack of famished wolves who pick off the dogs, one by one at night, get one of the men, and almost get the other. The point of view then shifts to the wolves and stays with them. Far from being a defect, the shift shows that the struggle for survival prevails in the same terms on all levels of life, with the same need for craft, strength, and courage. It is interesting to note, in this context, that Jack London wrote *The Call of the Wild* immediately after returning from his visit to London's East End, where he had seen society in the harshest terms of dog-eat-dog. Having established himself — largely with that book — he moved toward separating himself from society, buying more land than he could afford in order to have his own self-sufficient domain. In the beginnings of this withdrawal he wrote *White Fang*, symbolically projecting the lonely wolf into his own specially chosen world of love and security.

In *The Sea-Wolf* (1904) London ventured his second bout with a superior human being, this time a superman rather than a super-

woman. The story begins with Humphrey Van Weyden, a rather
delicate aesthete who has not been exposed to the harsh realities,
swept off a ferry crossing San Francisco Bay and presently rescued
by Captain Wolf Larsen of the sealing schooner *Ghost*. Humphrey,
forced to work as cabin boy, is on hand to study Wolf Larsen. He
is terribly strong, totally amoral, contemptuous of civilization's
slave morality. He is also something of an intellectual, close to
genius, who has read the philosophers and become an avowed
materialist. Humphrey finds his powers in atavism: "he is the perfect type of the primitive man, born a thousand years or genera-
tions too late and an anachronism in this culminating century of
civilization. . . . He was a magnificent atavism, a man so purely
primitive that he was of the type that came into the world before
the development of the moral nature." Wolf is a fascinating character. He may turn from reciting poetry or expounding philosophy to kick a troublesome sailor in the stomach; he sneers at God
and morals; and yet the sense of waste of his great powers compels
the reader's sympathy, as it does Humphrey's. A third of the book
is taken up with this exposition.

The plot begins when the *Ghost* picks up a handful of survivors
from a wreck. Among them is a beautiful, delicate, genteel poetess,
Maud Brewster. Humphrey, with high idealism, falls in love with
her; Wolf lusts after her with heartless egotism. Humphrey can
no longer be a spectator to Wolf's self-assertion. He escapes with
the poetess in a small boat and through stormy seas fetches an
island seal rookery in far northern waters. The lovers establish
themselves chastely in adjoining cottages and prepare to lay in
supplies of seal meat against the long winter. And now the dis-
mantled *Ghost* floats into their little harbor bearing only Wolf
Larsen, who has been abandoned by his crew. Humphrey could
kill him, but he is inhibited by his morality and by the force of
Wolf's personality. Wolf is having terrible headaches, and pres-

ently he goes blind. Humphrey sets about readying the *Ghost* to sail, but at night the blind Wolf gropes over the ship and destroys what Humphrey has done. In this suspenseful situation, while Humphrey is trying to summon the resolution to act, Wolf is stricken by paralysis — and presently dies.

The Sea-Wolf seems to turn into a different book with the appearance of Maud; the reason may be that it corresponded with a turning point in London's life. When he was halfway through writing the book, in 1903, he deserted Bess for Charmian Kittredge. Charmian, gushy, flirtatious, an intellectual chatterbox with a fine seat on a horse and an energetic social gaiety, set her traps for London and snared him. The relationship was kept secret for a long period during which the lovers exchanged volumes of fluttery, shrill, passionate letters. Charmian's style invaded Jack's style, and it was never quite the same again. Charmian is the model for Maud, "a delicate, ethereal creature, swaying and willowy, light and graceful of movement. It never seemed . . . that she walked, or, at least, walked after the ordinary manner of mortals. Hers was an extreme lithesomeness, and she moved with a certain indefinable airiness, approaching one as down might float or as a bird on noiseless wings." At about the same time, Charmian was writing to London, "Oh, you are wonderful — most wonderful of all. I saw your face grow younger under my touch. What is the matter with the world, and where do I belong. I think nowhere, if a man's heart is nowhere." And he wrote to her: "My arms are about you. I kiss you on the lips, the free frank lips I know and love. Had you been coy and fluttering, giving the lie to what you had already appeared to be by manifesting the slightest prudery or false fastidiousness, I really think I should have been utterly disgusted. 'Dear man, dear love!' I lie awake repeating those phrases over and over."

London has been roundly criticized for his treatment of Wolf

Larsen. Lewis Mumford says that instead of a higher type of human being, he created "a preposterous bully . . . little more than the infantile dream of the messenger boy or the barroom tough or the nice, respectable clerk whose muscles will never quite stand up under the strain. He was the social platitude of the old West, translated into a literary epigram." London later insisted that "the hurried superman of action" was doomed because he "is antisocial in his tendencies, and in these days of our complex society and sociology he cannot be successful in his hostile aloofness. . . . he acts like an irritant in the social body." This seems to be hindsight. Wolf Larsen had to be disposed of because of the new turn the book had taken, toward romantic love.

London later told the story of such a creature more consistently. *Burning Daylight* (1910) is about a comparable (if somewhat less intellectual) frontier superbrute. At one point he rushes into the office of the corporation that is cheating him and forces the squirming capitalists at gunpoint to do him justice. Here the hero represents a natural force asserting itself against the corruption and hypocrisy of the modern world; he gains sympathy and approval. Wolf too is presented as despising and defying the petty viciousness of a business-ridden society and the slave morality that sustains it; but once Maud Brewster took over the novel, London did not know what to do with him. The conflict with his crew or even with his soul (in the manner of a Captain Ahab) had to be abandoned. His reappearance at the seal island, stricken with blindness and paralysis, does not dramatize the forces presented earlier with so much intensity. The original Wolf could have become involved in an exciting and significant action.

Startling subjects, a bold narrative line, and the play of new ideas constitute London's appeal. As the years went by, his personal tie with his reader became an important element as well. He recognized the need for interesting material. He was always reading, meeting new people, and taking notes by the boxful. He was a tireless observer of events, situations, and matters of intellectual novelty. His famous Wednesday evening parties, attended by a parade of bums, grifters, cranks, and intellectuals, were not merely an indulgence, for these people were a source of characters and ideas. He even bought plots from the young Sinclair Lewis to bolster flagging invention. In his search for the unusual, the attention-catching, however, he increasingly moved too far from the representative concerns of men into the realm of fantasy. Without describing his works to tedium we may profitably follow this trend through a few of his stories, all written before 1906 (and all collected in a book of that year, *Moon-Face*).

An unsettling story, which joggles the bases of the social structure, is "The Minions of Midas" (1901). A multimillionaire is blackmailed for twenty million dollars by "members of [the] intellectual proletariat" who remind him that his wealth rests on power and declare that they will kill a designated person every week until he pays the sum demanded. He does not pay, "And week by week, as certain as the rising of the sun, came the notification and death of some person . . . just as much killed by us [the millionaire and his secretary] as though we had done it with our own hands." The millionaire holds out, disbursing "at the rate of one hundred thousand per week for secret service." As the murders continue, he increases it to a quarter of a million. He offers rewards totaling ten million dollars, but the murders continue. Then the symbolism is spelled out with a most ingenious ambiguity: "As I said before," the narrator explains, "a word from him and the slaughter would have ceased. But he refused to give that word. He insisted that the integrity of society was assailed; that he was not sufficiently a coward to desert his post; and that it was manifestly just that a few should be martyred for the ultimate welfare of the many." The narrator means by "a few" the people being murdered, but

28

the reader is forced to think of people sacrificed to make capitalism flourish — whether in sweatshop, industrial strife, or wars. The millionaire kills himself in anguish. And now the Minions of Midas speak more explicitly in another letter. They declare, "We are the inevitable. We are the culmination of industrial and social wrong. We turn upon the society that has created us. We are the successful failures of the age, the scourges of a degraded civilization. . . . We meet force with force. Only the strong shall endure." Capitalism has crushed wage slaves, shot strikers; now it is a free-for-all of power against power. So bold a stroke through the foundations of society must have been disturbing in 1901, although subsequent history has made it comparatively feeble.

Straight out of Edgar Allan Poe comes "Moon-Face" (1902), told by a man consumed with hatred for his jolly neighbor. The narrator kills his neighbor's dog, burns his barn, forecloses his mortgage, and finally commits the perfect crime. It is "William Wilson" and "The Cask of Amontillado" compressed into ten lively pages. Out of Mark Twain and the other humorists comes "The Leopard Man's Story" (1903) of how the knife thrower in a circus gets revenge on the lion tamer for looking at his wife. He drops some snuff on the lion tamer's hair, and when at the culmination of his act the latter puts his head in the lion's mouth, the lion sneezes and bites off his head with a *crunch*.

The infatuation with language so characteristic of the period, which seems to assume that anything is funny if it is told in three times as many words as necessary, overflows in "Local Color" (1903) in the account by a philosophical hobo of how he demonstrated that it would cost a town less to entertain a tramp in its best hotel than to arrest, convict, and incarcerate him for the same period. The hobo got thirty dollars for the story from a newspaper editor, put in some "local color" at the request of the editor who was pushing a campaign against the incumbent magistrate — and got sixty days in jail when haled before said magistrate after drinking up his thirty dollars in a brawl at the hoboes' haven. The picture of the magistrate had been too vivid.

Out of Poe, again, and the humorists comes "The Shadow and the Flash" (1903), a story about two brilliant rivals who become distinguished scientists. They compete desperately, whether for honors or women, until finally they take up the challenge of invisibility. One contends that there can be a black so black that it will be invisible because it reflects no light at all; the other seeks a chemical that will make him perfectly transparent. Both succeed, but the first when coated with his black paint has a shadow, and the second when made transparent by an injection emits a flash whenever the sun hits him from a certain angle. They come together in a final fury and kill each other in an invisible battle.

When the situations are this bizarre, the story leads to a conflict and choice likely to be equally bizarre; and the characterization which is the product of that choice will be fantastic. The jealous geniuses of "The Shadow and the Flash" cannot be taken seriously as people. And the same is true where the character is so enveloped in mystery that we can't know what makes him tick. For example, in "Planchette" (1906) a man endowed with godlike beauty and charm refuses after four years to disclose the mystery that prevents him from marrying the girl he deeply loves, who loves him as intensely. Two horses try to kill him. Then at a planchette (Ouija board) session, the spirit of the girl's father, who was a cavalry officer, promises to kill him. A day or so later another horse, famous for its steadiness, suddenly leaps over a cliff, carrying the man to his death. There is no explanation in this hair-raising tale, just suspense and mystery and a rich sensual throb that is sustained between the girl and the man up to a moment before his death. The assumption that the spirit of the father had some special influence over horses is not explanation enough.

Several qualities of *The Cruise of the Snark* (articles 1906–9, book 1911) strike the reader immediately. There is, first, the evidence that London has a public to whom he speaks directly and intimately. Like Mark Twain he assumes that the smallest detail of his life will be of interest. He talks about Charmian and Roscoe Eames (Charmian's uncle and nominal navigator on the *Snark*) by their first names as if the reader shared his connections with them. He builds suspense and emotional involvement for the reader over the question of how he (London) felt about every item in the calendar of delay and fraud that marked the building of the boat. A whole chapter tells how the months crept by while he lost bet after bet on his sailing date, spent $30,000, and was frustrated at every turn. The suspense grows from his original description of the wonderful Nova Scotia deck planks, the watertight compartments, the special engine, the power windlass, and all the custom-forged fittings to his successive discoveries that the planks were not full length, the compartments leaked, the engine was not secured properly (it broke loose from its bed and was carried to Hawaii as ballast), and the windlass and fittings were inferior (the windlass broke on first trial and the fittings snapped like matches). He maintains an air of happy trust and exuberance, leaving the reader to grind his teeth over the outrages London is suffering.

One feels here the pressures on a man trying to live three or four lives at once. Love, business, sailing, and debt consume London's time and vitality while forcing him to grind out his thousand words a day even if he has nothing to say. Thus a very little fact is stretched out over page after page with humorous repetition. We are told that the *Snark* won't heave to in a high wind; then this monstrous defect is rehearsed as every sail in the locker is tried. A whole chapter quotes letters from people all over the world who volunteered for the cruise. How London mastered the mysterious art of navigation in a couple of afternoons is told, then retold.

To sustain creation from almost nothing implies a powerful talent, and the more one reads the more one is struck by London's control of the language. He can evoke sharp images, explain complex procedures, describe intricate mechanisms and processes with economy and clarity. In Hawaii he does not merely admire the Kanakas surfing; he goes into the theory of wave motion and explains it in detail: "The face of that wave may be only six feet, yet you can slide down it a quarter of a mile, or half a mile, and not reach the bottom. For, see, since a wave is only a communicated agitation or impetus, and since the water that composes a wave is changing every instant, new water is rising into the wave as fast as the wave travels. You slide down this new water, and yet remain in your old position on the wave, sliding down the still newer water that is rising and forming the wave. You slide precisely as fast as the wave travels. . . . If you still cherish the notion, while sliding, that the water is moving with you, thrust your arms into it and attempt to paddle; you will find that you have to be remarkably quick to get a stroke, for that water is dropping astern just as fast as you are rushing ahead." This passage is an epitome of London's appeal: he involves the reader in an intellectual adventure that is just difficult enough to keep him alert with the effort to understand. The rush of thought is of a piece with the rush of discovery and adventure; here it surges along with the foaming racing sea. London not only draws the reader into the intellectual theory but also makes him participate in the adventurer's first incompetent attempts to master the skill. An intimacy is established thus and maintained through the book, as London enacts the reader's romantic dreams and timid impulses.

London's heart goes out to the lepers of Molokai, and he explodes the myth of their horror and despair by showing how active and happy they are in their colony. The description of the sixty-day passage, without sight of smoke or sail, from Hawaii to the

Marquesas rivals *Kon-Tiki*. At Nuka-hiva he follows Melville's footsteps into the Valley of Typee, to find those magnificent people almost exterminated by white men's diseases. The closing paragraph of this chapter, although it has one or two false notes, ends with a cadence that links it to the best of American prose: "The feast ended, we watched the moon rise over Typee. The air was like balm, faintly scented with the breath of flowers. It was a magic night, deathly still, without the slightest breeze to stir the foliage; and one caught one's breath and felt the pang that is almost hurt, so exquisite was the beauty of it. Faint and far could be heard the thin thunder of the surf upon the beach. There were no beds; and we drowsed and slept wherever we thought the floor softest. Near by, a woman panted and moaned in her sleep, and all about us the dying islanders coughed in the night."

As the party moves into the Solomons, they are overwhelmed with fever and various sores and infections; and so while the material grows richer, the ability of the author to handle it weakens. Hair-raising adventures are lost under the welter of medical detail. One wonders how the Londons survived this trip that was "all for fun." Jack in fact finally had to abandon the cruise and wound up with a long stay in an Australian hospital.

London drew heavily upon the romantic myth of himself for interest in his books. From the very first story of the Yukon, he was living violence, adventure, and triumph vicariously for the common reader. What is frankly central to the appeal of *The Cruise of the Snark* lurks in varying degrees very close to the surface in other books that his readers took as autobiography.

For London the living and writing became almost one, but it may be said that the writing really came first in the sense that it defined and directed the living. Just as the anguish of Hamlet's

> If thou dids't ever hold me in thy heart,
> Absent thee from felicity a while

33

> And in this harsh world draw thy breath in pain
> To tell my story

is unimaginable without the language in which it comes to us, so London's agonies had to be expressed if they were to achieve fullness and intensity. Hamlet of course lives only in the poetry. There he only is. But the same is almost true of a Jack London. He exists in his books as he writes, as he expresses, as he discovers the meanings and intensities for which he could not even yearn without language. He grows in the books and lives his evolving role between them, as the man in the flesh enacts the man in the books. London's biographers comment in surprise on the fact that he could be almost dead with thirst on the becalmed *Snark* and stagger down to the cabin to write a story about a sailor dying of thirst. But he had to write the experience before he really knew it.

The interest in *Martin Eden* (1909) is richest if we read the book to see what sort of sense London could make of the intellectual and psychological materials that he knew best in himself. The long "novel" begins with an uncouth sailor entering the luxurious home of a cultured friend (whom he has, characteristically, saved from a gang of toughs). His wide shoulders and lurching walk make a space large enough for six people seem too narrow; he breaks out into a sweat of anxiety. An amused glance from the friend "burned into him like a dagger-thrust," for "under that muscled body of his he was a mass of quivering sensibilities." The exposition proceeds to show a mind of dazzling intensity that jumps from the present event to evoke brilliant images of past experience. While he talks painfully to the friend's ethereal sister (Ruth Morse), scenes of brawls, whores, engine rooms, prisons, and wild seas surge and tumble before his mind's eye. The excitement grows in a new dimension as the frail girl responds — and is shocked by her response — to his superb body while she is horrified by his grammar.

Martin Eden is famished for knowledge, power, life — and the story plunges straight into his quest for them. He goes on to great successes, to disillusion, to suicide. But the struggles surging through the mind of the author break the confines of the single story he had to write and so confuse the characterization of the hero. London was indignant with his notices and said, "Not one blessed reviewer has discovered that this book is an attack on individualism, that Martin Eden died because he was so utter an individualist that he was unaware of the needs of others, and that, therefore, when his illusions vanished, there was nothing for him for which to live." This sentence may describe London better than his hero, for while creating his self-destructive individualist London was also creating and exploring the mystery of his own famished spirit that could never rest while it could never be satisfied, because it did not understand (and could not understand) that its trouble was rooted in his fatherless, homeless, famished childhood. And London edits his own life in ways that tell more than he could have realized. The anemic Mabel Applegarth is transformed into a Ruth Morse who is beautiful and proud and harries Martin Eden because he is not respectably employed. Jack broke with Mabel because she could not get free from her dominant mother. Money was not the problem. Ruth breaks her engagement when Martin is reported in the press as having made a flaming socialist speech (falsely, for it was a Nietzschean attack on socialism). Bessie Maddern does not appear in the book. And Ruth evolves somewhat. Late in the story she offers to become Martin's mistress so that she can convince him of her sincerity and persuade him to marry her. This is a disguised Charmian London, who did indeed seduce Jack and then lured him away from Bessie by holding herself at a distance until he got his divorce. Charmian was five years older than Jack; Ruth is three years older than Martin.

Martin Eden turns into a daydream of prowess, wish-fulfillment, and revenge. London's own problems are transmuted into glories of beauty, strength, and intelligence pitted against supernal outrages. His face "was once as white as the underside of his arm; nor did he dream that in the world there were few pale spirits of women who could boast fairer or smoother skins than he — fairer than where he had escaped the ravages of the sun." As, fired by love, he begins to educate himself, "She detected unguessed finenesses in him . . . and was often puzzled by the strange interpretations he gave to mooted passages [in Browning's poetry]. It was beyond her to realize that, out of his experience of men and women and life, his interpretations were far more frequently correct than hers. . . . He was tortured by the exquisite beauty of the world . . . He was drunken with unguessed power," which is not only creative but also physical, for "The old familiar blaze of health rushed out from him and struck her like a blow. It seemed to enter into her body and course through her veins in a liquid glow, and to set her quivering with its imparted strength." Inspired by her, "he spent the day in the white-hot fever of re-creating the beauty and romance that burned in him." Hints of megalomania abound, as when "he rented a typewriter, and spent a day mastering the machine" — rather in the manner that the young Mozart is said at the age of six to have picked up a violin and performed a part in his father's string quartet.

The romance with Ruth, floating on his inchoate but enraptured vision of the beauty of the world, bumps against her cultured disdain for excess — which is, however, not able to suppress her physical response to his electrifying power. "Mentally she was in a panic to shoot the bolts and drop the bars into place, while wanton instincts urged her to throw wide her portals and bid the deliciously strange visitor to enter in." She would like to kill the male in him and yet have it too, but under her genteel control and guided into profitable and respectable channels. Consciously, however, she recoils from physical contact with a man who has lived through the imagined and unspeakable evils of a sailor's world. Finally her mother-dominated spirit gives in to her burgeoning womanhood and she discovers a passionate (but of course chaste) love for Martin, even though she remains spiritually absorbed, self-centered, uncommunicating, hoping he will give up his mad writing and get a steady job.

Martin toils on, knowing that he is Ruth's intellectual superior, as he also knows that inspiration alone is not enough and that his genius must be supported by knowledge. Now "His was deliberate creative genius, and, before he began a story or poem, the thing itself was already alive in his brain, with the end in sight, and the means of realizing that end in his conscious possession." His studies led to a synthetic essay. "It was brilliant, deep, philosophical, and deliciously touched with laughter. . . . The writing of it was the culminating act of a long mental process, the drawing together of scattered threads of thought, and the final generalizing upon all the data with which his mind was burdened." Such ability and application should have been recognized, but the weeks of heroic toil went on and on, while the rejection slips accumulated and the money dwindled until Martin had nothing but potatoes to eat. He was out of his head with starvation and fever when the big letter came (not from the *Black Cat* as in London's life, but from the *White Mouse*) offering him $40 for a story.

The action of this novel drags along as Martin's intellectual explorations are spelled out, for these are used to represent the period of his apprenticeship, in place of London's own Klondike adventures, months on the road and in prison, assault on high school and university, and days at sea. The effect is to make the period of his self-education more concentrated and intense than the corresponding years of London's life, but also much more

37

limited in activities. The debaters, socialists, and professors in
Eden's life are met at Ruth Morse's home, and he is more than
a match for them all, even for the most brilliant professor in the
university, whose intellect he diagnoses as deficient in biological
insights. "Professor Caldwell sat for a full minute, silent and
fingering his watch chain. 'Do you know,' he said at last, 'I've had
that same criticism passed on me once before — by a very great
man, a scientist and evolutionist, Joseph Le Conte. But he is dead,
and I thought to remain undetected; and now you come along and
expose me.'" The rest of the upper class Martin considers para-
sites, but he is aligned with them because he is an avowed individualist, not, as London thought he himself was, a socialist.

He does not stay on their side, however, because he rapidly sees
what shams and leeches they are. In ruthless discussions with pomp-
ous bankers and judges at the Morses' dinner table, he confutes
them with facts and abuses them with eloquence. He makes one
brilliant insight here into the future of American politics. "'You
persuade yourself,'" he tells the judge, "'that you believe in the
competitive system and the survival of the strong, and at the same
time you endorse with might and main all sorts of measures to
shear the strength from the strong. . . . It's on record, your position on interstate commerce regulation, on regulation of the rail-
way trust and Standard Oil, on the conservation of the forests,
on a thousand and one restrictive measures that are nothing else
than socialistic.'" These predictions, milder than the prophecy
of world fascism in *The Iron Heel*, are much nearer the truth —
although they are not essentially different.

Eden meets an incomparably brilliant nihilist named Brissenden, who argues that the critics, the publishers, and especially
the magazines are despicable haters and destroyers of literature.
Brissenden writes the greatest poem of the century ("It was a
mad orgy of imagination, wassailing in the skull of a dying man

who half sobbed under his breath and was quick with the wild flutter of fading heart-beats"), which he refuses to sully by publication. He begs Martin to give up his quest for wealth via the contemptible magazines: " 'Love beauty for its own sake . . . and leave the magazines alone. Back to your ships and your sea — that's my advice to you, Martin Eden. What do you want in these sick and rotten cities of men? You are cutting your throat every day you waste in them trying to prostitute beauty to the needs of magazinedom. If you got [fame] it would be poison to you. You are too simple, too elemental, and too rational, by my faith, to prosper on such pap. . . . It is not in what you succeed in doing that you get your joy, but in the doing of it. . . . Beauty hurts you. It is an everlasting pain in you, a wound that does not heal, a knife of flame. Why should you palter with magazines?' " Brissenden expresses what Martin believes with increasing conviction, but this is very far from the real Jack London, who always wrote for the market and bragged of doing so. Martin Eden, too, studies the magazines to discover the formula of success; his later despair over the public's failure to appreciate the utter passionate beauty of his work is as phony as a three-dollar bill. London's wish-fulfillment makes Martin's motivation inconsistent, his characterization a failure.

Brissenden takes Martin to an enclave in the slums where a group of intellectuals who have renounced the bitch-goddess success and all that goes with "respectability" engage in far-ranging discussions that embrace all knowledge. The words describing the brilliance of these men are as excessive as the actual discussion is sophomoric: "He swiftly saw, no matter upon what they talked, that each man applied the correlation of knowledge and had also a deep-seated and unified conception of society and the Cosmos . . . Never had Martin, at the Morses', heard so amazing a range of topics discussed. . . . Martin was struck by the inside knowledge they possessed. They knew what was never printed in the newspapers — the wires and strings and the hidden hands that made the puppets dance." The debate ranges Locke, Berkeley Hume, Kant, Spencer, and Haeckel against each other through two pages of highfalutin oversimplification. It provides the perfect footnote to the statement that London was an uneducated man of genius.

At a socialist meeting, Martin brilliantly expounds the Nietzschean attack on socialist slave morality which protects the weak and prevents evolutionary development. He is reported in the papers as a socialist; Ruth breaks their engagement; he is denounced by his neighbors, his family, and the tradesmen who have given him credit. Brissenden commits suicide, leaving Martin alone and really at the end of his rope. He is in a daze of exhaustion, despair, disappointed love, and, most of all, utter disillusion with the stupidity of critics and intellectuals.

Then a long-overdue check comes, and Martin uses it to send out all his manuscripts for a final try at the market. Success! They are accepted one after another and the money comes in faster than Martin can spend it. A book of philosophy (forsooth!) causes a sensation, sells sixty thousand copies; the publisher sends a blank contract for anything he has either planned or written and responds with a check for $5000 when he writes a title on the blank line. His first and second books now top the best-seller list, week after week, "thus proving himself to be that rare genius, a critic and a creator in one." Still numb, he forgives his enemies, buys a milk farm for his kind Portuguese landlady, allows himself to be interviewed by the reporter who wrote him up as a socialist, and accumulates a fortune without writing another line.

As Martin turns the other cheek to one indignity after another (he finances the two brothers-in-law who forbade him their homes), the effect is of a childish, sulky daydream of revenge. He is an angry infant breaking his toys to spite the grownups. He broods incessantly over the fact that the work was all performed when he was a lonely outcast; now the stinking world wallows at his feet while he smiles in tight-lipped disdain. Ruth's attempt to seduce him is an ultimate abasement that lets him pour out all his disgust for "bourgeois vulgarity." But the question he keeps asking with such tormented intensity — "And what is puzzling me is why they want me now. Surely they don't want me for myself, for myself is the same old self they did not want" — is a question to which he has known the answer all his life: they want him for his fame and his money. Anybody knows that. It's so obvious that it's not worth saying; it makes the ending painfully false; the suicide becomes an act of sulky spite, of childish pique.

Martin Eden has been considered London's best work, but I believe it is among his worst. It lacks aesthetic distance; it lacks the sense of control that comes when a writer has *made* a book. Its author is nakedly, naively, embarrassingly present in its situations. The best of London is to be found in the short stories, *The Call of the Wild*, and *White Fang*.

Burning Daylight (1910) is cut from the same cloth. London plays the Viking hero bearding the pigs of capitalists and making them eat crow; he is heroic as socialist and as individualist. *John Barleycorn* (1913) is an incantation, a solemn ritual of exorcism. London writes in the first person to explain the perils of drink and to tell how he conquered it. The book is wish-fulfillment, for London was far gone in alcoholism when he wrote it and was to be a physical ruin in a year or two more. The psychology of alcoholism is profoundly — if unconsciously — revealed in this book. *The Valley of the Moon* (1913) concentrates on the struggle of a young couple through the social jungle and on to where they leave society and become scientific farmers in their private valley. This book is full of Anglo-Saxon racism, a misbegotten offspring

41

of Darwin and the notion that only a pure breed could be strong. *The Little Lady of the Big House* (1916) is all about Jack and Charmian and Wolf House. Into their Eden comes a friend from Yale who unintentionally falls in love with the heroine. She then finds herself in love with both men. The hero insists that she make a choice freely, and the story descends into bathos; yet one cannot avoid the impression that the sentimental death of the heroine represents Jack's growing impatience with his jealous, frilly, demanding, and irresponsible wife.

London contributed greatly to one myth of the American writer, which he passed from Mark Twain on to F. Scott Fitzgerald and Ernest Hemingway. All these writers (and the line extends thinly back to Poe) tried to live several lives at once and in the attempt sacrificed their lives, their art, or their peace to the excess they attempted. London is like Mark Twain in his grandiose and disastrous business schemes. He was like Fitzgerald in alcoholism and in his involvement with a woman who took so much of his life that she invaded his art. He was like Hemingway in his boyishness, his two-fisted courage, his public display of dangerous living, and even his great capacity for friendship. Like the others, he seemed always to be in a desperate struggle with his writing, so that the extra activities might be regarded as symptoms rather than causes of their frustration.

The classic book about this problem is Van Wyck Brooks's *The Ordeal of Mark Twain*. Brooks maintains that Twain, with an incomparable genius, was frustrated by Puritanism, by frontier distrust of excellence which forced him to be a funny man, and finally by his own sellout to the Gilded Age, which disastrously compromised his art. Brooks says that Twain would have had to become a great satirist if he was to fulfill himself and defeat the Gilded Age. London, in a similar state, did become a satirist. He spent his life discovering and castigating abuses of every sort, from

apitalism in all its corrupt manifestations, through organized
religion, and on even to bullfighting. And he was confused and
frustrated in the same way that Mark Twain was.

It may be suggested that the root of this problem is not what
Brooks claims, but is rather the absence in America of an established society that could be taken seriously by the artist because
in its manners, customs, and values he found problems about
which he could write a rich and steady flow of serious novels of
manners. Or perhaps one should say either the absence of such a
society or the absence of a *tradition* of taking it seriously. Once
a writer like London or Twain has uttered his wild assault on the
stupidity of society in general, he is out of material. He must go
to the Klondike, or back to the Middle Ages, or into boys' stories,
or through the green hills of Africa with rod, gun, and pen, or
down into the South Seas; or contrive hoaxes like *Tom Sawyer
Abroad*; or bring the devil himself down to discuss what man is;
or make fun of Europe; or create a popular myth of himself to
exploit. With exotic subjects and intellectual protest he will have
the greatest difficulty making plots that move seriously through
the center of society, and therefore he will not generally be able
to create characters that are representative. They will instead
be burlesques, outlaws, brutes, Indians, children, or adventurers.

To make the point by way of contrast, one may look at the
career of J. P. Marquand. He did find American society, with all
its defects, worth his sustained and serious attention. He was able
to write one long book after another dealing with various problems of that society, problems of war, business, love, and so on,
that moved right through the heart of American life. Marquand
has generally been considered a writer just below the first rank,
but the point here is that he was always interesting, always serious,
and never in the least danger of running out of materials. It is
significant, in passing, that Marquand began with satires —*The*

Late George Apley and *H. M. Pulham, Esq.* — but abandoned thi
tone apparently because its burlesque note faded quickly.

Jack London never wrote a novel of manners, never took th
patterns of American society seriously, never found typical prob
lems in it with which he could wholeheartedly engage himsel
His stories of the Klondike are valid because the Gold Rush wa
an actual experience of Americans in an actual part of the con
tinent; the Darwinian struggle for survival was at that time ;
foremost preoccupation in American thought. His socialist writ
ings are often moving because they take us into areas of miser
and deprivation with which modern man is deeply concerned
but this stream soon runs into the sands, compelling the autho
to invent new fantasies of violence or prophecy. These element:
place London in the naturalistic movement, which embraces sci
entific determinism, Darwinism, the Spencerian philosophy of evo
lution, and Marxism, all of which in some way reflect the anti
supernaturalism and anti-traditionalism of a presumably scientifi
approach to human affairs. These all theoretically (although neve
in practice) renounce the free will and ethical responsibility tha
underlay the classic well-made novel of manners — and thus con
tribute to the restless search for form that has characterized the
American novel since 1900.

London's special genius appears in his command of detail an
pace. He knows how to produce realism and suspense by giving
the minutest factual items of a situation — and how on the othe
hand to jump over large areas of fact and make the reader supply
the information or the meaning. He can bring the most seasoned
sophisticate to the edge of his chair and have him fidgeting with
anxiety as a story builds toward its climax. A good introduction
to London is the three-volume *Bodley Head Jack London*. Read
ing this collection of his best in novels and stories, one must
acknowledge that that best is very good indeed.

✗ *Selected Bibliography*

Works of Jack London

NOVELS AND COLLECTIONS OF SHORT STORIES

The Son of the Wolf, Tales of the Far North. Boston: Houghton, Mifflin, 1900.
The God of His Fathers and Other Stories. New York: McClure, Phillips, 1901.
A Daughter of the Snows. Philadelphia: Lippincott, 1902.
Children of the Frost. New York: Macmillan, 1902.
The Call of the Wild. New York: Macmillan, 1903.
The Faith of Men and Other Stories. New York: Macmillan, 1904.
The Sea-Wolf. New York: Macmillan, 1904.
The Game. New York: Macmillan, 1905.
Moon-Face and Other Stories. New York: Macmillan, 1906.
White Fang. New York: Macmillan, 1906.
Before Adam. New York: Macmillan, 1906.
Love of Life and Other Stories. New York: Macmillan, 1906.
The Iron Heel. New York: Macmillan, 1907.
Martin Eden. New York: Macmillan, 1909.
Lost Face. New York: Macmillan, 1910.
Burning Daylight. New York: Macmillan, 1910.
When God Laughs and Other Stories. New York: Macmillan, 1911.
Adventure. New York: Macmillan, 1911.
South Sea Tales. New York: Macmillan, 1911.
The House of Pride and Other Tales of Hawaii. New York: Macmillan, 1912.
Smoke Bellew Tales. New York: Century, 1912.
A Son of the Sun. New York: Doubleday, Page, 1912.
The Night-Born. New York: Century, 1913.
The Abysmal Brute. New York: Century, 1913.
The Valley of the Moon. New York: Macmillan, 1913.
The Strength of the Strong. New York: Macmillan, 1914.
The Mutiny of the Elsinore. New York: Macmillan, 1914.
The Scarlet Plague. New York: Macmillan, 1915.
The Star Rover. New York: Macmillan, 1915.
The Little Lady of the Big House. New York: Macmillan, 1916.
The Turtles of Tasman. New York: Macmillan, 1916.
The Human Drift. New York: Macmillan, 1917.
The Red One. New York: Macmillan, 1918.

On the Makaloa Mat. New York: Macmillan, 1919.
Hearts of Three. New York: Macmillan, 1920.
Dutch Courage and Other Stories. New York: Macmillan, 1922.
The Assassination Bureau, Ltd. (completed by Robert L. Fish). New York:
  McGraw-Hill, 1963.

PLAYS

Scorn of Women. New York: Macmillan, 1906.
Theft. New York: Macmillan, 1910.
The Acorn-Planter. New York: Macmillan, 1916.

ESSAYS, TRACTS, TRAVEL, AUTOBIOGRAPHY, LETTERS

The Kempton-Wace Letters (with Anna Strunsky). New York: Macmillan, 1903.
The People of the Abyss. New York: Macmillan, 1903.
War of the Classes. New York: Macmillan, 1905.
The Road. New York: Macmillan, 1907.
Revolution and Other Essays. New York: Macmillan, 1910.
The Cruise of the Snark. New York: Macmillan, 1911.
John Barleycorn. New York: Century, 1913.
Letters from Jack London, edited by King Hendricks and Irving Shepard. New
  York: Odyssey Press, 1965.

JUVENILES

The Cruise of the Dazzler. New York: Century, 1902.
Tales of the Fish Patrol. New York: Macmillan, 1905.
Jerry of the Islands. New York: Macmillan, 1917.
Michael, Brother of Jerry. New York: Macmillan, 1917.

RECENT SELECTED EDITION

The Bodley Head Jack London, edited by Arthur Calder-Marshall. 3 vols.
  London: Bodley Head, 1963–64.

CURRENT AMERICAN REPRINTS

The Assassination Bureau, Ltd. (with R. L. Fish). New York: McGraw-Hill.
  $1.95.
The Best Short Stories of Jack London. New York: Premier Books (Fawcett).
  $.60.
Brown Wolf and Other Jack London Stories. New York: Acorn Books (Mac-
  millan). $.79.

urning Daylight. New York: Popular Library. $.35.

he Call of the Wild. New York: Airmont. $.50. New York: Companion (Grosset and Dunlap). $1.25. Boston: Riverside (Houghton, Mifflin). $.92. Englewood Cliffs, N.J.: Scholastic Book Services. $.50. New York: Washington Square Press. $.60.

he Call of the Wild and Selected Stories. New York: Signet (New American Library). $.50.

he Call of the Wild and White Fang. New York: Bantam. $.45. New York: Washington Square Press. $.45.

he Iron Heel. New York: American Century (Hill and Wang). $1.45.

ack London: Short Stories, selected by Maxwell Geismar. New York: American Century. $1.75.

Iartin Eden. New York: Holt, Rinehart, and Winston. $1.25.

he Mutiny of the Elsinore. New York: Popular Library. $.35.

he Sea-Wolf. New York: Airmont. $.50. New York: Bantam. $.50. Boston: Riverside. $1.25.

he Sea Wolf and Selected Stories. New York: Signet. $.60.

outh Sea Tales. New York: Pyramid Books. $.50.

Vhite Fang. New York: Airmont. $.50. New York: Washington Square Press. $.60.

Bibliography

There is no adequate bibliography for London. "A Jack London Bibliography" appears in Charmian London, *The Book of Jack London* (New York: Macmillan, 1921), II, 397–414. Bibliographical information may also be found in Joseph Gaer's *Jack London* (Monograph No. 1 of California Literary Research Project, 1934) and J. Haydock's "Jack London: A Bibliography of Criticism," *Bulletin of Bibliography*, 23:42–46 (May–August 1960).

Critical and Biographical Studies

Feied, Frederick. *No Pie in the Sky: The Hobo as American Cultural Hero in the Works of Jack London, John Dos Passos and Jack Kerouac*. New York: Citadel, 1964.

Foner, Philip S. *Jack London: American Rebel*. New York: Citadel, 1947, 1964.

Geismar, Maxwell. *Rebels and Ancestors*. Boston: Houghton, Mifflin, 1953, Pp. 139–216.

Herrick, Robert. *The Memoirs of an American Citizen*. New York: Macmillan, 1905.

James, George W. "A Study of Jack London in His Prime," *Overland Monthly*, 69:361–99 (May 1917).

Johnson, Martin. *Through the South Seas with Jack London*. New York: Dodd, Mead, 1913.

Lane, R. W. "Life and Jack London," a serial in *Sunset* extending from October 1917 to May 1918.

London, Charmian. *The Book of Jack London*. 2 vols. New York: Century, 192

———. *The Log of the Snark*. New York: Macmillan, 1915.

———. *Our Hawaii*. New York: Macmillan, 1917; revised edition, 1922.

London, Joan. *Jack London: An Unconventional Biography*. New York: Doubleday, 1939.

McDevitt, William. *Jack London as Poet*. San Francisco: Recorder-Sunset Press, 1947.

Mencken, H. L. *Prejudices: First Series*. New York: Knopf, 1921. Pp. 236–3.

Mumford, Lewis. *The Golden Day: A Study in American Literature and Culture*. New York: Boni and Liveright, 1926. Pp. 247–50.

Noel, Joseph. *Footloose in Arcadia: A Personal Record of Jack London, George Sterling, Ambrose Bierce*. New York: Carrick, 1940.

O'Connor, Richard. *High Jinks on the Klondike*. Indianapolis: Bobbs, Merrill, 1954.

———. *Jack London: A Biography*. Boston: Little, Brown, 1964.

Pattee, Fred L. *Side-Lights on American Literature*. New York: Century, 192. Pp. 98–160.

Payne, Edward B. *The Soul of Jack London*. London: Rider, 1926.

Schorer, Mark. *Sinclair Lewis: An American Life*. New York: McGraw-Hill, 1961. Pp. 164–66 and *passim*.

Stone, Irving. *Sailor on Horseback*. Boston: Houghton, Mifflin, 1938. Reissued as *Jack London, Sailor on Horseback: A Biographical Novel*. New York: Doubleday, 1947.

Walcutt, Charles Child. *American Literary Naturalism, a Divided Stream*. Minneapolis: University of Minnesota Press, 1956. Pp. 87–113.

Williams, Blanche C. *Our Short Story Writers*. New York: Moffat, Yard, 1920. Pp. 256–57.